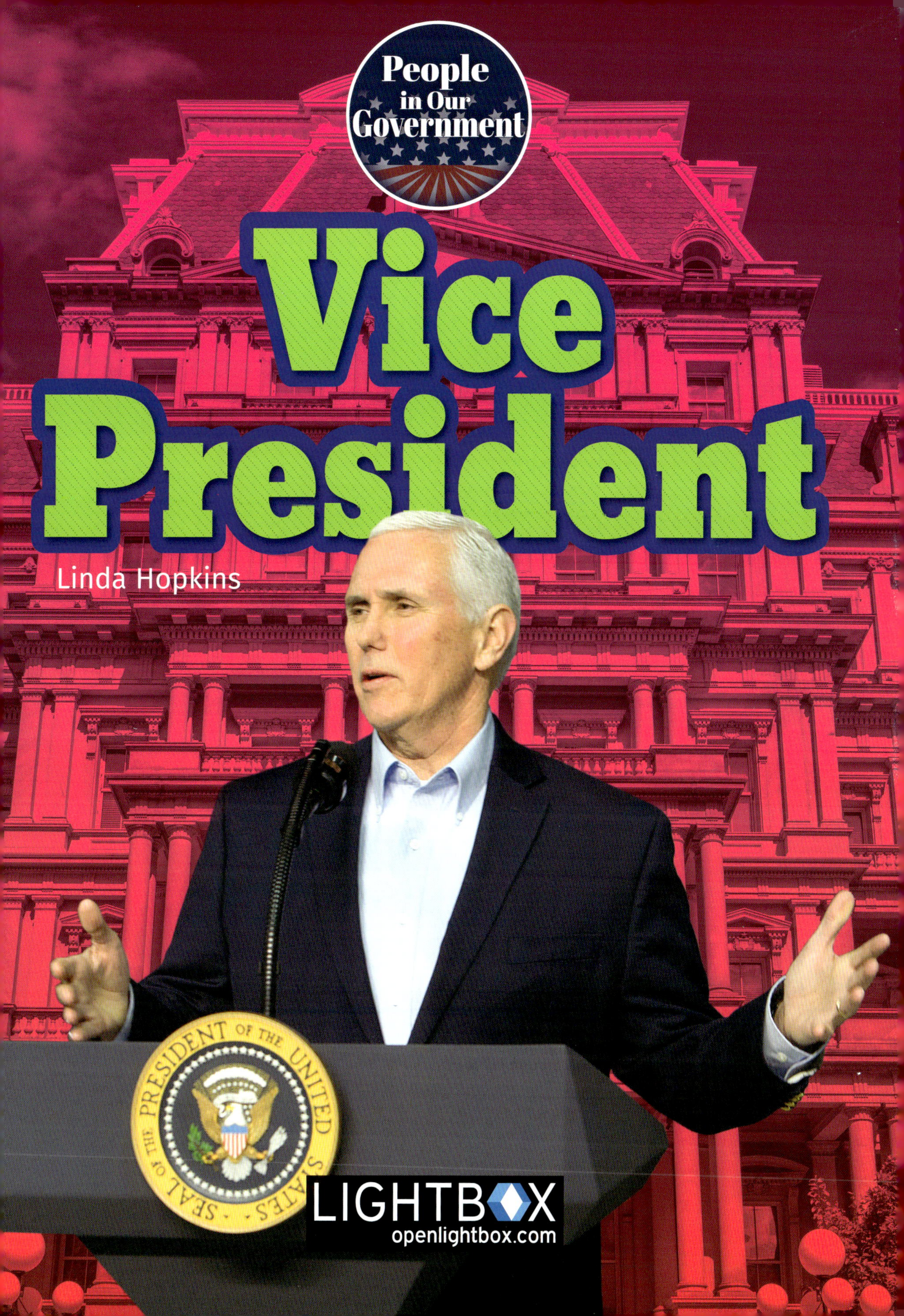
People in Our Government
Vice President
Linda Hopkins
SEAL OF THE PRESIDENT OF THE UNITED STATES
LIGHTBOX
openlightbox.com

Go to
www.openlightbox.com
and enter this book's
unique code.

ACCESS CODE

LBXZ7896

Lightbox is an all-inclusive digital solution for the teaching and learning of curriculum topics in an original, groundbreaking way. Lightbox is based on National Curriculum Standards.

STANDARD FEATURES OF LIGHTBOX

AUDIO High-quality narration using text-to-speech system

ACTIVITIES Printable PDFs that can be emailed and graded

SLIDESHOWS Pictorial overviews of key concepts

VIDEOS Embedded high-definition video clips

WEBLINKS Curated links to external, child-safe resources

TRANSPARENCIES Step-by-step layering of maps, diagrams, charts, and timelines

INTERACTIVE MAPS Interactive maps and aerial satellite imagery

QUIZZES Ten multiple choice questions that are automatically graded and emailed for teacher assessment

KEY WORDS Matching key concepts to their definitions

Vice President

Contents

Who Is the Vice President?

The vice president of the United States is the second-in-command to the president. The vice president helps the president do his or her job. If a president is removed from office, the vice president becomes president.

The first U.S. vice president was John Adams. Before he became vice president, he was a leader of the **American Revolution**. He later became the second U.S. president.

John Adams came in second place during the first presidential election. In those times, the person who came in second became the vice president.

The Government

The U.S. government is described in the Constitution. This document was written to establish the new country and its laws. The Constitution explains the three branches of government. Each branch has its own role. Together, they take care of the country and its people.

The legislative branch makes the country's laws. The executive branch carries out the laws. The judicial branch settles any problems with the country's laws.

The executive branch is based in the White House in Washington, D.C.

Structure of the U.S. Government

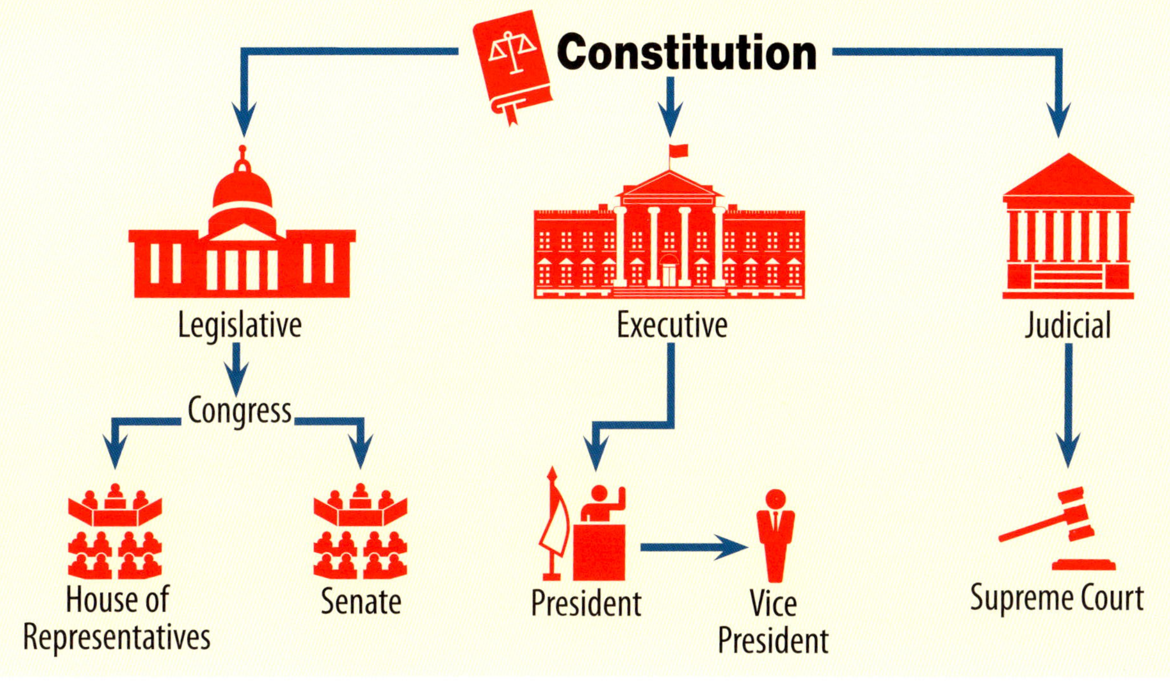

The Role

The vice president gives the president advice on issues affecting the country. He or she is also first in the line of **succession**. This means that if the president can no longer do his or her job, the vice president will take over. Vice President Lyndon B. Johnson became the president when President John F. Kennedy was **assassinated** in 1963.

The vice president is also the president of the Senate. The Senate is part of the legislative branch of the government. As president of the Senate, the vice president gets the deciding vote in a tie. If there are the same number of votes for an issue, he decides which side will win. If the vice president is not able to be at Senate meetings, the Senate **elects** a **president pro tempore** to do the job instead.

Lyndon B. Johnson was sworn in as president while on an airplane.

Theodore Roosevelt became president when President William McKinley was assassinated. Eight presidents have died or been assassinated in office.

Vice presidents have made **268 tie-breaking votes.**

A **vice president** has taken over the role of president **9 times.**

John C. Breckinridge is the only vice president who ever fought against the U.S. government. He was on the opposing side during the Civil War.

What It Takes

There are certain rules someone must meet in order to become vice president. He or she must have been born in the United States and be a U.S. **citizen**. The vice president must be at least 35 years old and have lived in the country for at least 14 years.

John C. Breckinridge became vice president when he was 36 years old. He is the youngest vice president. Alben Barkley is the oldest vice president. He was 72 years old when his term began.

A statue of Alben Barkley stands at the Kentucky State Capitol. Before he was vice president, he served as a member of Congress.

Getting the Job

The vice president is elected every four years. The vice president is part of a team with the president. There are several steps to becoming vice president.

1 Presidential **candidates** from each **political party** travel the country to gain support. Party members in each state choose the candidate they want to be president.

2 Large meetings are held. Each political party chooses one person who will run for president.

3

The chosen candidate picks a **running mate** who **campaigns** with him or her to be elected.

4

People across the country vote for the team they think should be president and vice president. Their votes are called the popular vote.

5

Each state has people called electors. The votes of the electors decide who becomes president and vice president. Each state's electoral votes go to the team with the highest popular vote in that state. The team with the most electoral votes overall becomes president and vice president.

The Eisenhower Executive Office Building

The vice president has three offices. One is in the West Wing of the White House. This is where the vice president does most of his or her work. There is also an office in the U.S. Capitol, where the Senate meets. The third office is across the street from the White House in the Eisenhower Executive Office Building.

The Law Library
The president of the United States and other members of the executive branch use this library.

It took **17 years** to build the **Eisenhower Executive Office Building.**

The Eisenhower Executive Office Building originally had **553 rooms** and **151 fireplaces.**

Diplomatic Reception Room
Many important events with foreign leaders take place in this room on the south wing's second floor.

Indian Treaty Room
Located on the fourth floor of the east wing, this room is used for meetings, receptions, and certain **swearing-in ceremonies** for members of the government.
The Vice President's Ceremonial Office
The vice president uses this second-floor office in the east wing when he or she has interviews with the press.

Leading in Public

The vice president helps the president lead the country. He or she steps in to run meetings or give speeches when the president is not available. The vice president also travels around the country to meet people and understand more about what they want from their government.

The vice president joins state governors to talk about issues affecting that state.

Represents the President

The vice president shares the president's ideas. He or she often travels around the United States to give speeches. The vice president meets with many people and groups.

Advises the President

The vice president advises the president. He or she often has a background in certain political topics. For example, a vice president may be knowledgeable about public health or the environment.

The president invites the vice president to attend meetings in the Oval Office, which is the president's office in the White House.

In the Senate, the vice president announces electoral vote results for the presidential elections.

Leads the Senate

The vice president is the president of the Senate. This means he or she can lead Senate meetings. Vice presidents performed this job more often in the past. Today, the vice president usually only attends Senate meetings when there may be a tied vote.

Meets with World Leaders

The vice president meets with leaders of other countries. This can be to strengthen relationships and increase **trade**. Joe Biden visited 57 countries in the eight years he was vice president.

Vice President Dick Cheney traveled to the Middle East several times to meet with leaders and discuss the ongoing war in the region.

A Day in the Life

The vice president's job has changed over the years. The first vice presidents mainly ran the Senate meetings. They did not have their own projects to lead. More recent vice presidents have busy schedules and issues that they work on independently.

Vice President Mike Pence hosts groups at the Eisenhower Executive Office Building for special events, such as honoring members of the military and their families.

8:00 am

The vice president meets with the president to discuss the day.

9:30 am

The vice president travels to Detroit, Michigan. He tours a manufacturing plant and meets with employees.

2:00 pm

Back in Washington, D.C., the vice president holds a **press conference** to announce a new trade agreement.

3:30 pm

The vice president leads a Senate meeting as senators discuss the appointment of a new judge.

6:00 pm

He takes a call from Canada's minister of international trade to discuss sending goods from the United States to Canada.

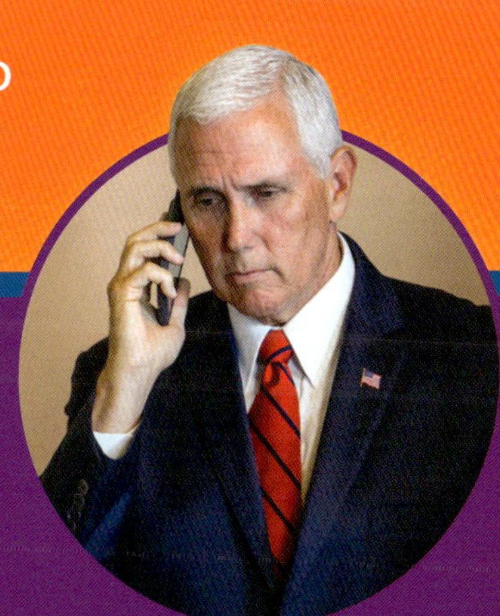

8:00 pm

The vice president talks to the president on the phone to discuss the day's events.

Notable Vice Presidents

Presidents choose their running mates for different reasons. Some vice presidents have skills or knowledge that balance the president's experience. Many vice presidents have played an important role in the country's development.

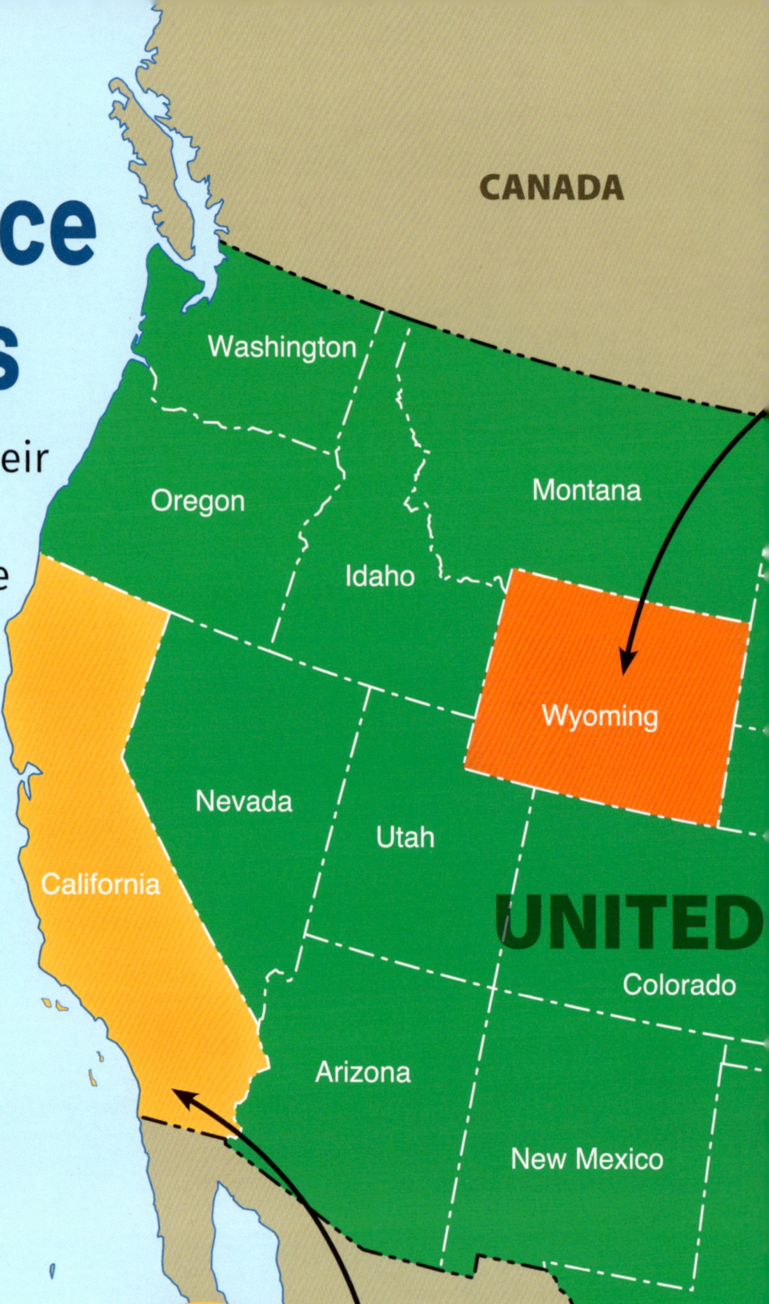

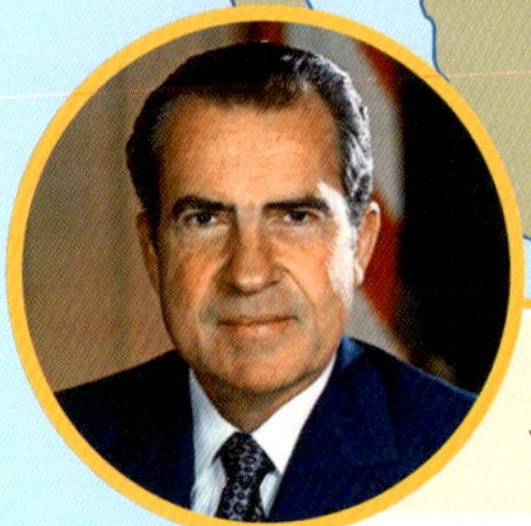

CANADA
Washington
Oregon
Montana
Idaho
Wyoming
Nevada
Utah
California
UNITED
Colorado
Arizona
New Mexico
Pacific
Ocean
MEXICO
Texas

Hawai'i
Scale
100 Miles
0 100 Kilometers

Alaska
Scale
500 Miles
0 500 Kilometers

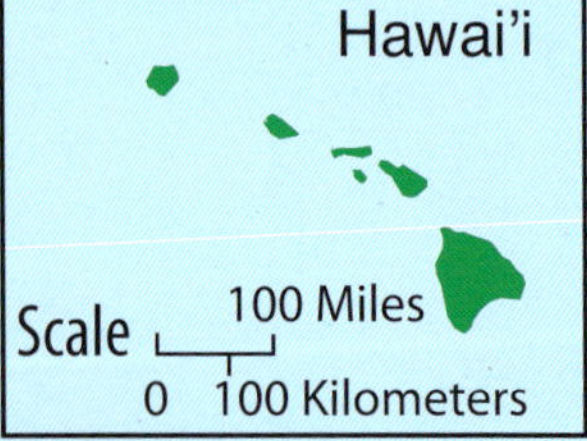

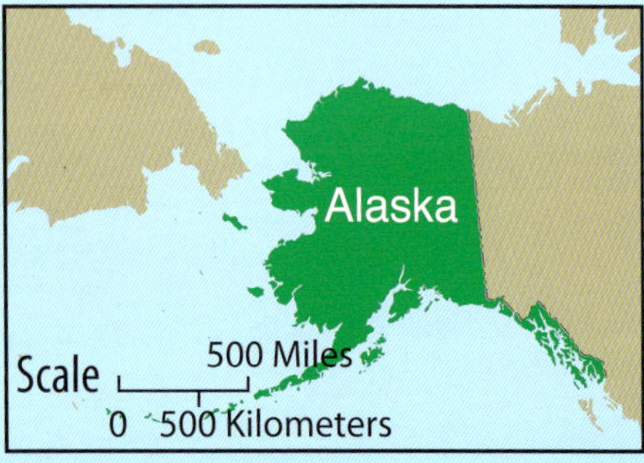

Richard M. Nixon
Years in Office: 1953–1961

Nixon was the 36th vice president of the United States. He later became the 37th president. Nixon was the first vice president to serve as an international **goodwill ambassador**.

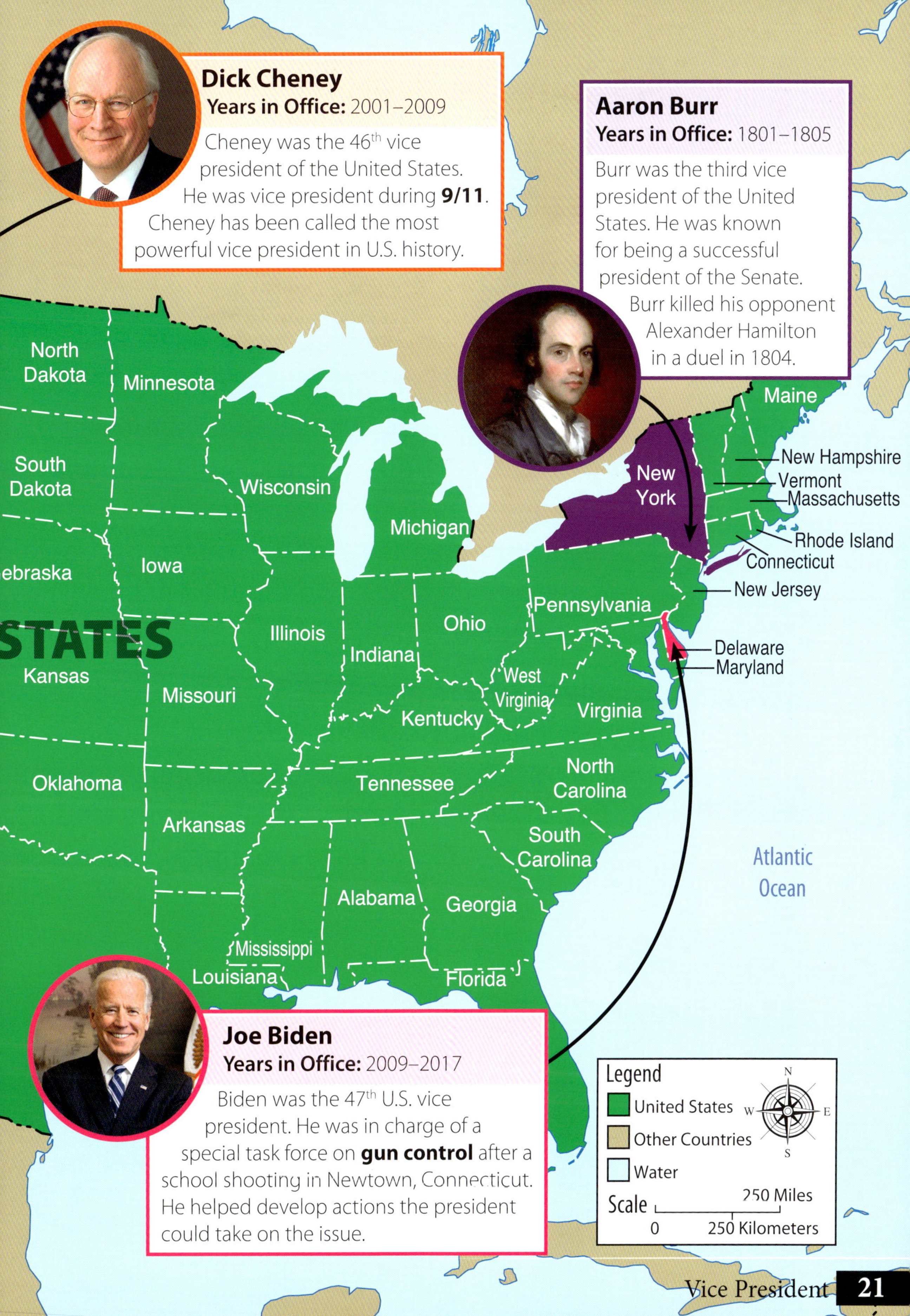

Dick Cheney
Years in Office: 2001–2009
Cheney was the 46th vice president of the United States. He was vice president during 9/11. Cheney has been called the most powerful vice president in U.S. history.
Aaron Burr
Years in Office: 1801–1805
Burr was the third vice president of the United States. He was known for being a successful president of the Senate. Burr killed his opponent Alexander Hamilton in a duel in 1804.
North Dakota
Minnesota
South Dakota
Wisconsin
Michigan
New York
Maine
New Hampshire
Vermont
Massachusetts
Rhode Island
Connecticut
New Jersey
ebraska
Iowa
STATES
Illinois
Indiana
Ohio
Pennsylvania
Delaware
Maryland
Kansas
Missouri
West Virginia
Kentucky
Virginia
Oklahoma
Tennessee
North Carolina
Arkansas
South Carolina
Atlantic Ocean
Alabama
Georgia
Mississippi
Louisiana
Florida
Joe Biden
Years in Office: 2009–2017
Biden was the 47th U.S. vice president. He was in charge of a special task force on gun control after a school shooting in Newtown, Connecticut. He helped develop actions the president could take on the issue.
Legend
United States
Other Countries
Water
N
W
E
S
Scale
0
250 Miles
250 Kilometers

Quiz

1 Who was the first vice president of the United States?

2 The Senate is part of which branch of the U.S. government?

3 Who was the vice president when John F. Kennedy was assassinated?

4 How old must someone be to become vice president?

5 What is the name of the building where the vice president has his ceremonial office?

6 Which vice president was the first to serve as an international goodwill ambassador?

ANSWERS

1 John Adams **2** Legislative **3** Lyndon B. Johnson **4** 35 years old
5 Eisenhower Executive Office Building **6** Richard M. Nixon

Key Words

9/11: stands for the terrorist attacks of September 11, 2001, when four planes flew into the World Trade Center in New York, the Pentagon in Arlington, Virginia, and a field in Pennsylvania, killing almost 3,000 people

American Revolution: the war in which the American colonies broke free of British rule

assassinated: murdered for political reasons

campaigns: makes an effort to become elected

candidates: people who seek or are put forward for a job

citizen: a person who lives in a particular country and legally belongs to that country

elects: votes into a job

goodwill ambassador: a person who travels to different places to promote friendship

gun control: the set of laws that controls the sale of firearms

political party: a group of people who share the same views about the way power should be used in a country

president pro tempore: president for a time

press conference: an event organized to provide information and answer questions from the media

running mate: a person running together with another person for two closely related government roles

succession: the process of inheriting a title or office

swearing-in ceremonies: official events where people make a promise to do their job

trade: the business of buying and selling goods

Index

LIGHTBOX

SUPPLEMENTARY RESOURCES

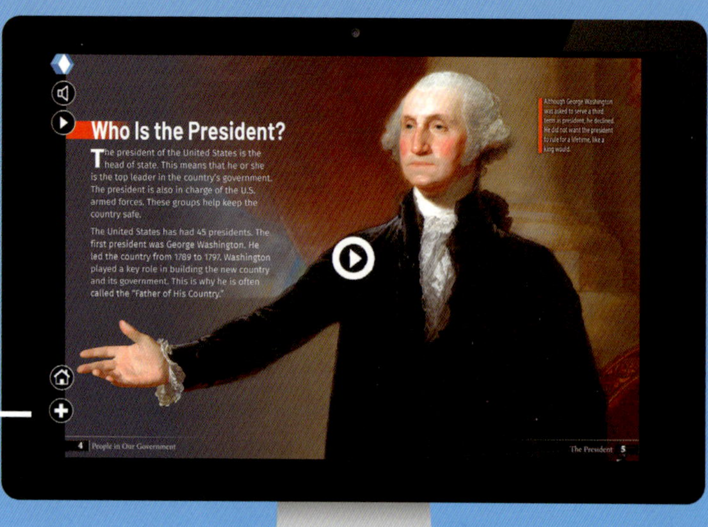

Click on the plus icon ⊕ found in the bottom left corner of each spread to open additional teacher resources.

- Download and print the book's quizzes and activities
- Access curriculum correlations
- Explore additional web applications that enhance the Lightbox experience

LIGHTBOX DIGITAL TITLES
Packed full of integrated media

VIDEOS

INTERACTIVE MAPS

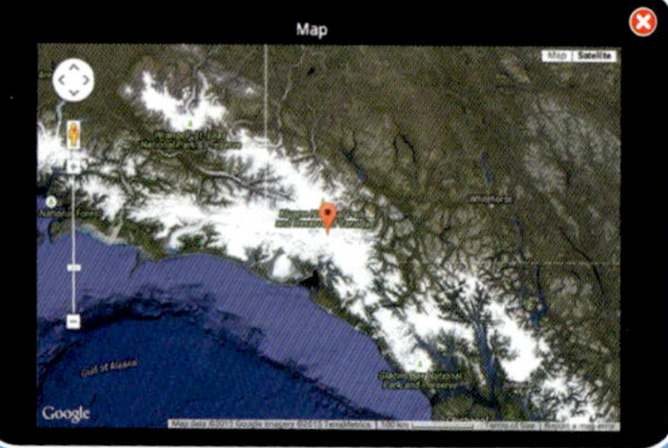

WEBLINKS

SLIDESHOWS

QUIZZES

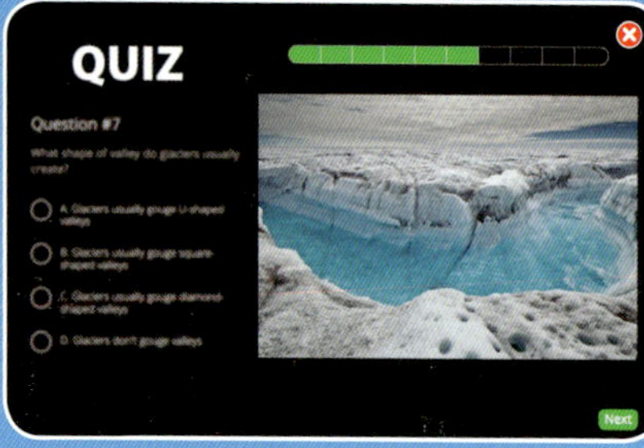

OPTIMIZED FOR

- ✓ TABLETS
- ✓ WHITEBOARDS
- ✓ COMPUTERS
- ✓ AND MUCH MORE!

Published by Smartbook Media Inc.
14 Penn Plaza 9th Floor
New York, NY 10122
Website: www.openlightbox.com

Library of Congress Control Number: 2020938420

ISBN 978-1-5105-5458-0 (hardcover)
ISBN 978-1-5105-5459-7 (multi-user eBook)

Printed in Guangzhou, China
1 2 3 4 5 6 7 8 9 0 24 23 22 21 20

062020
111019

Project Coordinator Heather Kissock
Designer Ana María Vidal

Photo Credits
Every reasonable effort has been made to trace ownership and to obtain permission to reprint copyright material. The publisher would be pleased to have any errors or omissions brought to its attention so that they may be corrected in subsequent printings. The publisher acknowledges Alamy, Getty Images, and iStock as its primary image suppliers for this title.